I0559939

WINTER THINGS..

Christmas

© Cathy McGough 2025

First published in October, 2025.

All Rights Reserved. No part of this publication may be reproduced or transmitted in any form or by any means, electronic or mechanical, including photocopy, recording or any other information storage and retrieval system, without prior permission in writing from the publisher at Stratford Living Publishing.

ISBN Print: 978-1-998651-85-6

Cathy McGough has asserted her right under the Copyright, Designs and Patents Act, 1988 to be identified as the author of this work.

Art powered by Canva Pro.

This is a work of fiction. The characters in it are all fiction. Resemblance to any persons living or dead is purely coincidental. Names, characters, places and incidents either are the products of the author's imagination or are used fictitiously.

Dedicated to Kate

ZEBRA

I dream of running in a marathon...
Because there's a zebra inside of me.
I run alongside my zebra family and friends...
Together we make the world more stripe-y!

"Do the stripes make us run faster?" I ask...
Of the zebra who lives inside of me.
He says, "I don't think so mate...
But it sure helps with our camouflage-ry!"

"I'm just a kid and even I know, that's a made up word!" I explain.
The zebra laughs, tickling my tummy.
"Words aren't a zebra kind of thing!" he says...
"But our thing is OUTRUNNING our enemies!"

"Fair enough!" I say. "Me? I only run for fun!"
The zebra says, "For us zebras, running keeps us free!"
He and the other zebras form a dazzle and run...
Soon their stripe-y-ness is all I can see!

REINDEER

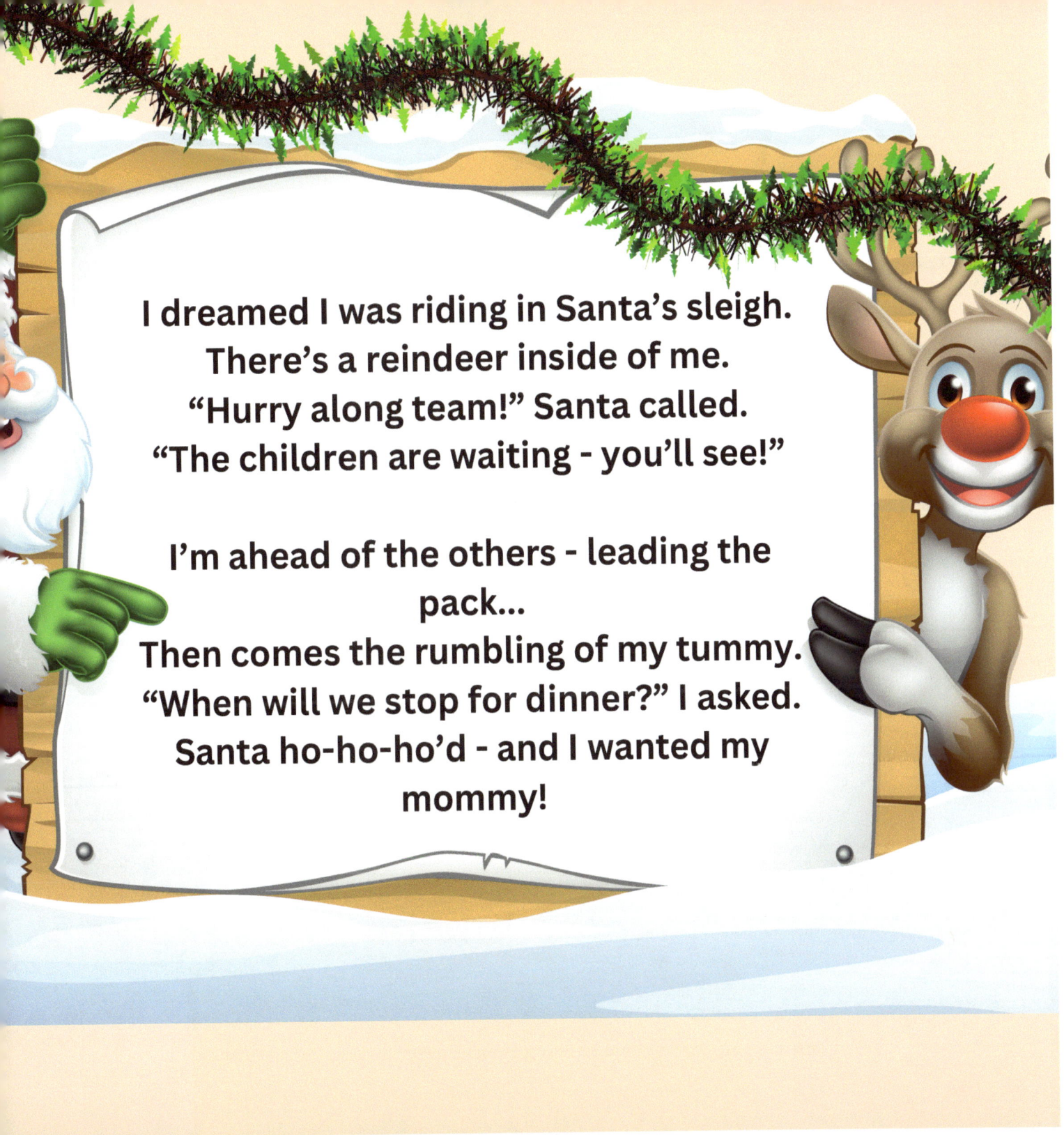

I dreamed I was riding in Santa's sleigh.
There's a reindeer inside of me.
"Hurry along team!" Santa called.
"The children are waiting - you'll see!"

I'm ahead of the others - leading the pack...
Then comes the rumbling of my tummy.
"When will we stop for dinner?" I asked.
Santa ho-ho-ho'd - and I wanted my mommy!

I heard Santa behind us chuckling away...
Then he tossed smelly reindeer treats into the air.
We caught what we could and munch, munch
munched!
Happily bringing gifts to children everywhere!

CHRISTMAS CAROLE

I keep singing Christmas songs!
That's because there is a Christmas Carole inside of me!
Carole knowns the words to every Christmas song!
And she sings and teaches them to me!

Some Christmas songs make me laugh...
Some make me sad and I want to cry.
Others inspire me to wrap presents...
A few make me want to decorate low and high!

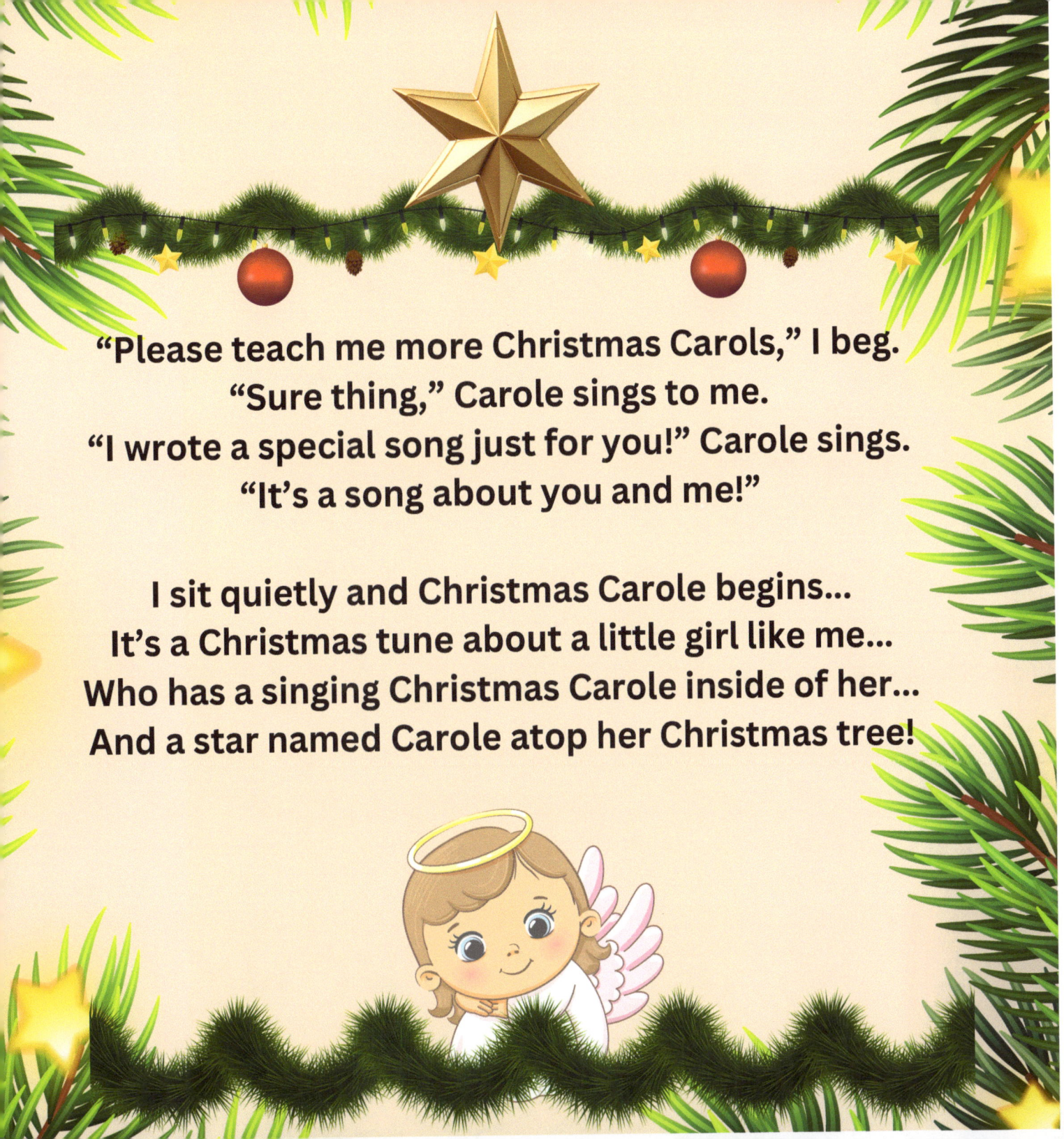

"Please teach me more Christmas Carols," I beg.
"Sure thing," Carole sings to me.
"I wrote a special song just for you!" Carole sings.
"It's a song about you and me!"

I sit quietly and Christmas Carole begins...
It's a Christmas tune about a little girl like me...
Who has a singing Christmas Carole inside of her...
And a star named Carole atop her Christmas tree!

SHETLAND PONY

Riding with a team of ponies on a cold winter day...
Because I have a Shetland Pony inside of me.
We gallop and our hooves crunch down the snow...
Pulling a sleigh is happy work for us ponies.

I am sitting in the sleigh, between mommy and daddy.
We have warm blankets covering our knees.
"Come up here! Climb upon my shoulders!" says
The Shetland Pony who lives inside of me.

Then like magic, I am on my pony's back...
And sitting between mommy and daddy too!
It's fun to be in two places at once...
When there's a Shetland Pony living inside of you!

CAMEL

I wonder what it was like way back then...
Because there's a camel inside of me.
To follow the Star in the sky all across the desert...
To travel with The Three Kings like a V.I.P.

Carrying the gifts of gold, frankincense and myrrh...
Bringing the gifts to give to the Baby.
I feel like a king, but I'm just a camel...
Through the eyes of the camel I can see.

The star above us, leads our Camel Caravan...
On the way to meet the special baby.
Even though he isn't born yet all know His name...
And how important to the world He will be.

The camel through whose eyes I see...
Kneels down and Baby Jesus smiles at me.
We celebrate Jesus, every day of the year...
On Christmas Day we celebrate his birthday.

DOVE AND CARDINAL

A dove is a bird of peace.
A cardinal is a bird of hope.
Both exist inside of me...
It's Christmas Eve around the globe.

We trim the tree with beautiful treasures...
The red cardinal's hue stands out.
The pure whiteness of the dove...
Casts peaceful vibes throughout.

The cardinal and the dove yearn to soar!
And spread the messages they carry far and wide...
But on Christmas they are content to remain...
And share in the warmth we provide.

CANDY CANES

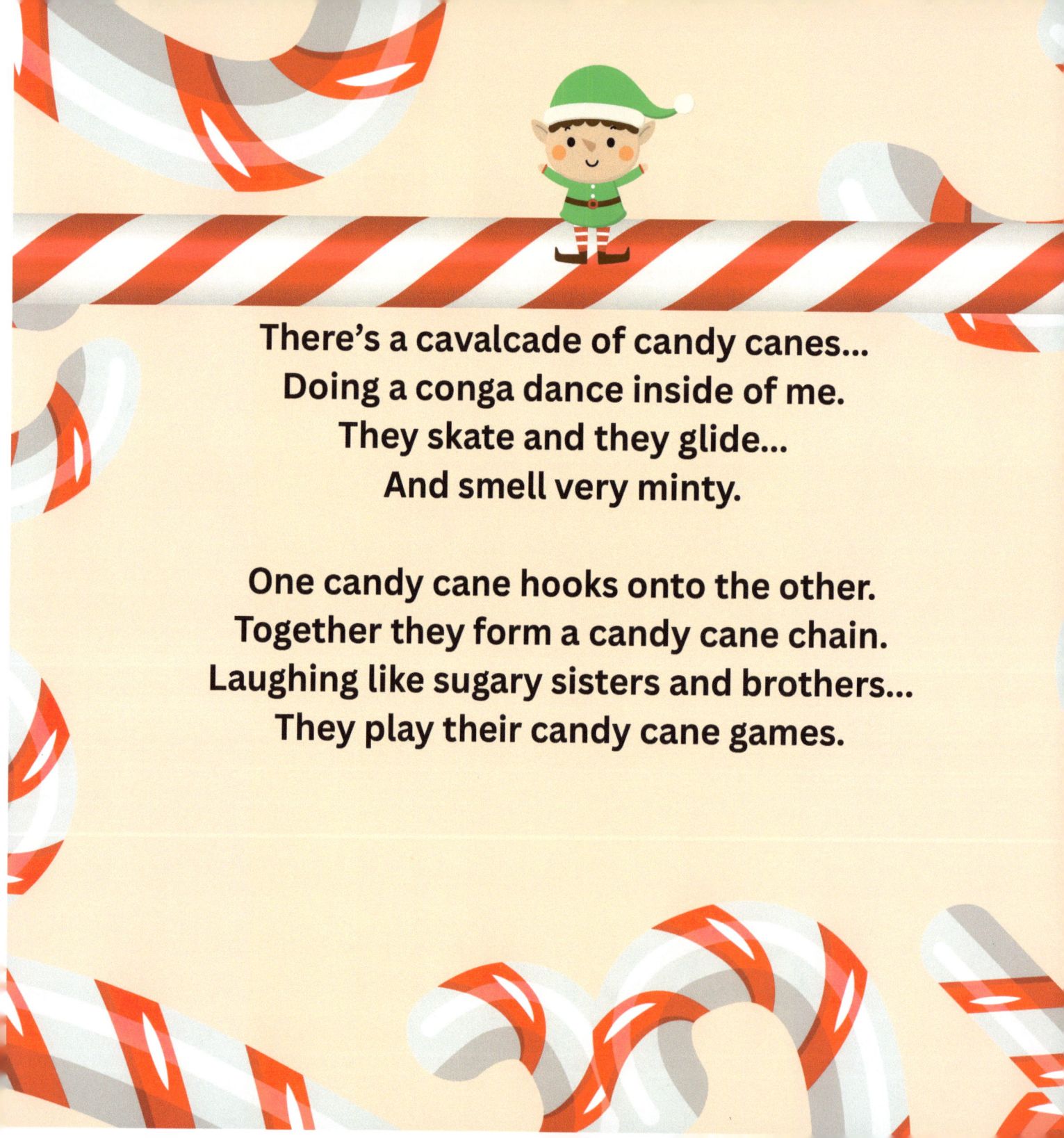

There's a cavalcade of candy canes...
Doing a conga dance inside of me.
They skate and they glide...
And smell very minty.

One candy cane hooks onto the other.
Together they form a candy cane chain.
Laughing like sugary sisters and brothers...
They play their candy cane games.

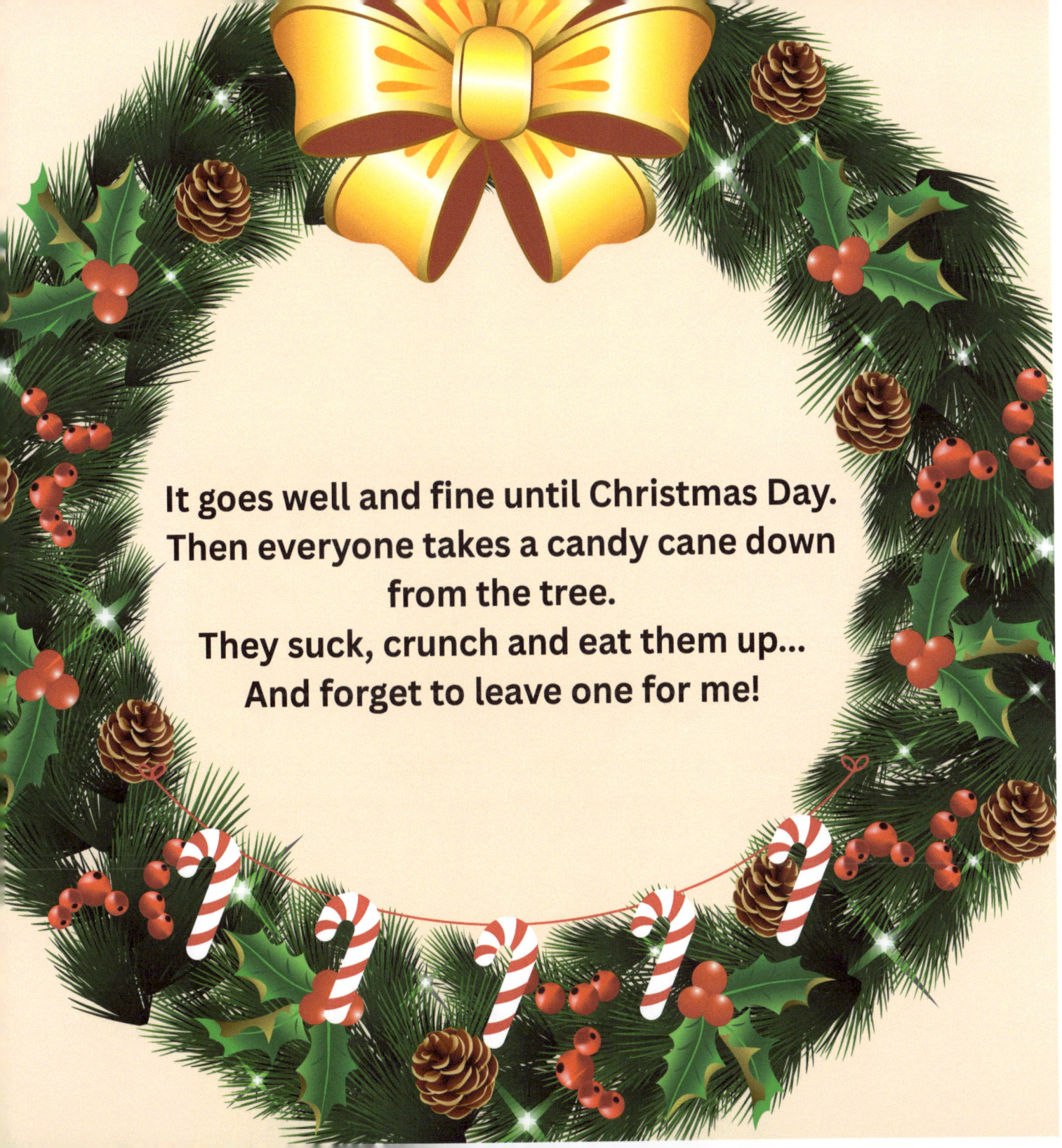

It goes well and fine until Christmas Day.
Then everyone takes a candy cane down
from the tree.
They suck, crunch and eat them up...
And forget to leave one for me!

CHRISTMAS TRAIN

Climb aboard the Christmas Train!
Get ready to cross the country!
Imagine the sights you will see...
Through the windows of the Christmas Train inside of me!

On your left is a town with a stable outfront...
And behind it there is a Steeple.
Christmas Eve Mass will be held there soon...
Let's wave to all the people!

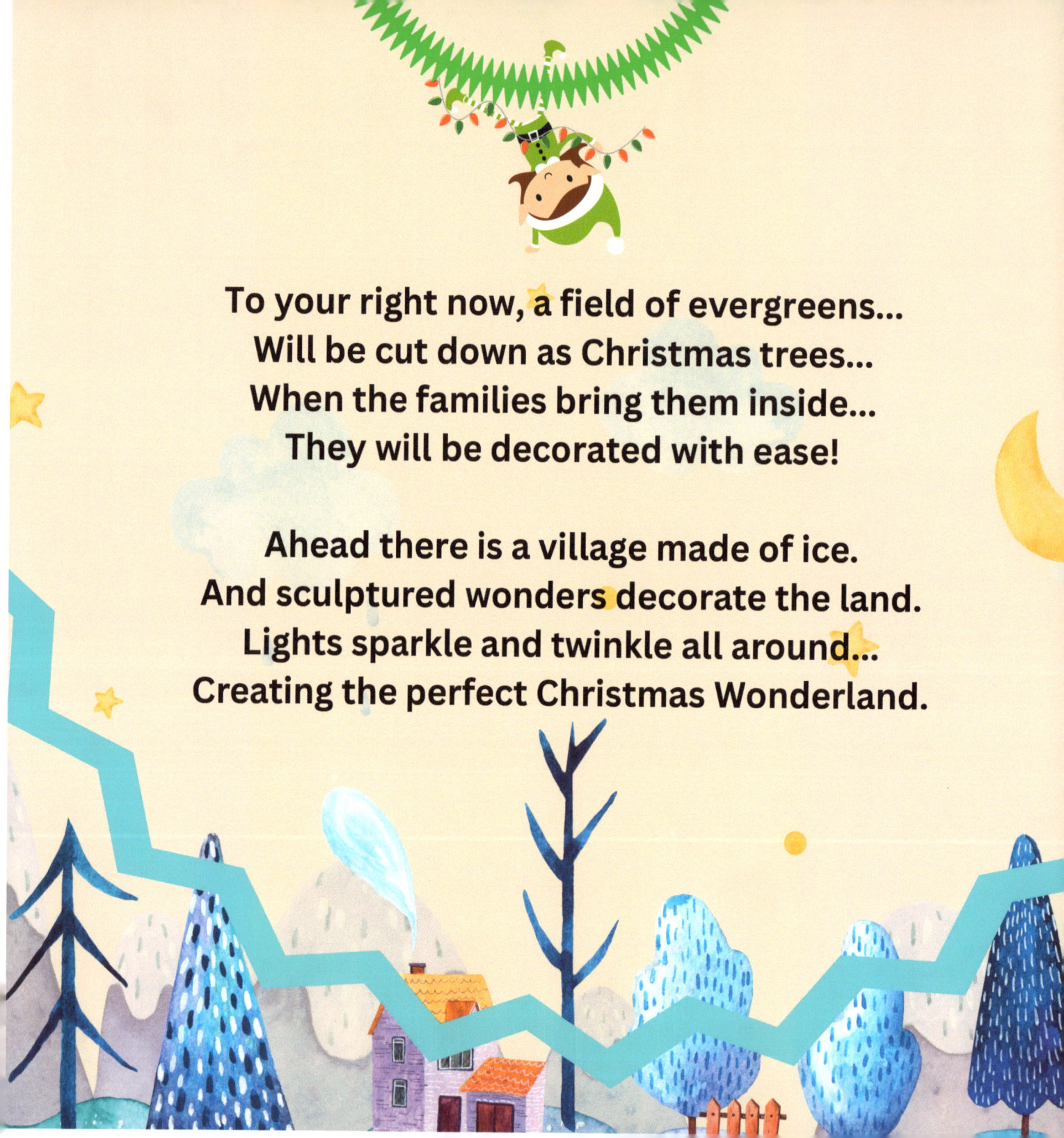

To your right now, a field of evergreens...
Will be cut down as Christmas trees...
When the families bring them inside...
They will be decorated with ease!

Ahead there is a village made of ice.
And sculptured wonders decorate the land.
Lights sparkle and twinkle all around...
Creating the perfect Christmas Wonderland.

The Christmas Train's whistle blows...
Because I'm sleepy an angel descends...
"Happy Christmas little one!" she sings...
As the Christmas Train ride ends.

TOBOGGAN

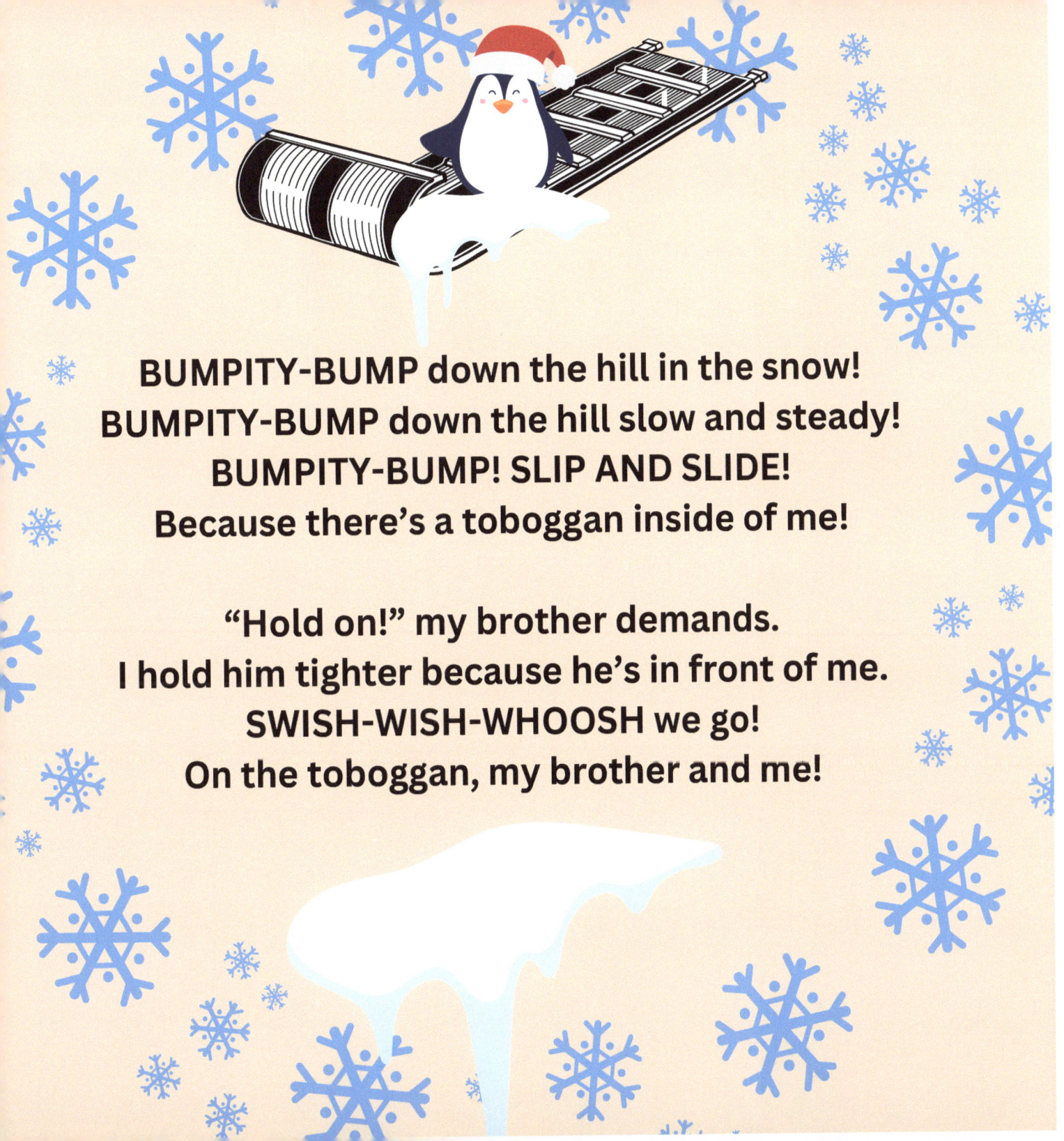

BUMPITY-BUMP down the hill in the snow!
BUMPITY-BUMP down the hill slow and steady!
BUMPITY-BUMP! SLIP AND SLIDE!
Because there's a toboggan inside of me!

"Hold on!" my brother demands.
I hold him tighter because he's in front of me.
SWISH-WISH-WHOOSH we go!
On the toboggan, my brother and me!

When we get to the bottom...
The toboggan whips the snow into our eyes!
We laugh and shake it off!
Then climb back up the hill for another try!

This time my brother tells me to get on first...
I check with the toboggan inside of me.
He giggles, then whispers as I get on...
We begin sliding before my brother grabs onto me!

"Just because he's older..."
Says the toboggan inside of me.
"Your brother should still follow the rules.
Rules are meant for all age safety!"

I see my brother covered in snow and shivering...
I run to him, and replace his wet hat with mine.
"Thanks, Bro!" he says to me with a grin.
I help him stand, and back up the snowhill we climb!

SILLY SAUSAGES AND
CHRISTMAS CRACKERS

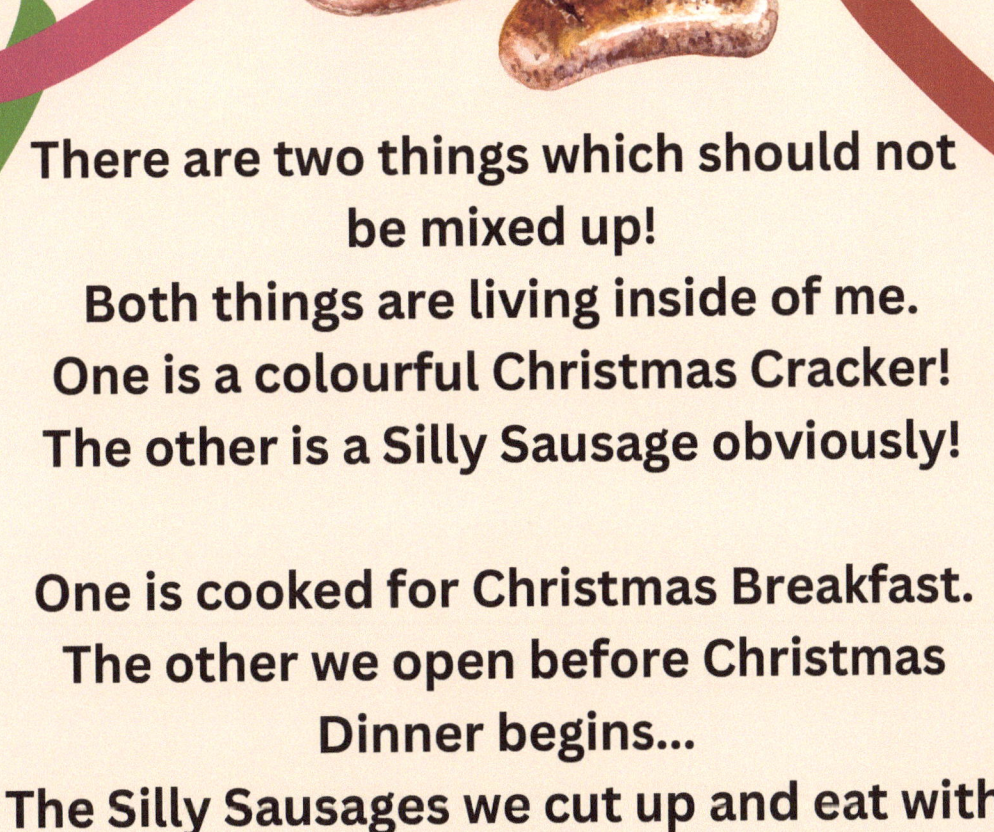

There are two things which should not be mixed up!
Both things are living inside of me.
One is a colourful Christmas Cracker!
The other is a Silly Sausage obviously!

One is cooked for Christmas Breakfast.
The other we open before Christmas Dinner begins...
The Silly Sausages we cut up and eat with eggs.
When we pull a Christmas Cracker every one wins!

The Silly Sausages are only silly...
When they laugh as they are sizzling
in the pan.
Whereas the Christmas Crackers
often fail to crack...
We all wear our Christmas Cracker
hats - except for my Nan!

LOON

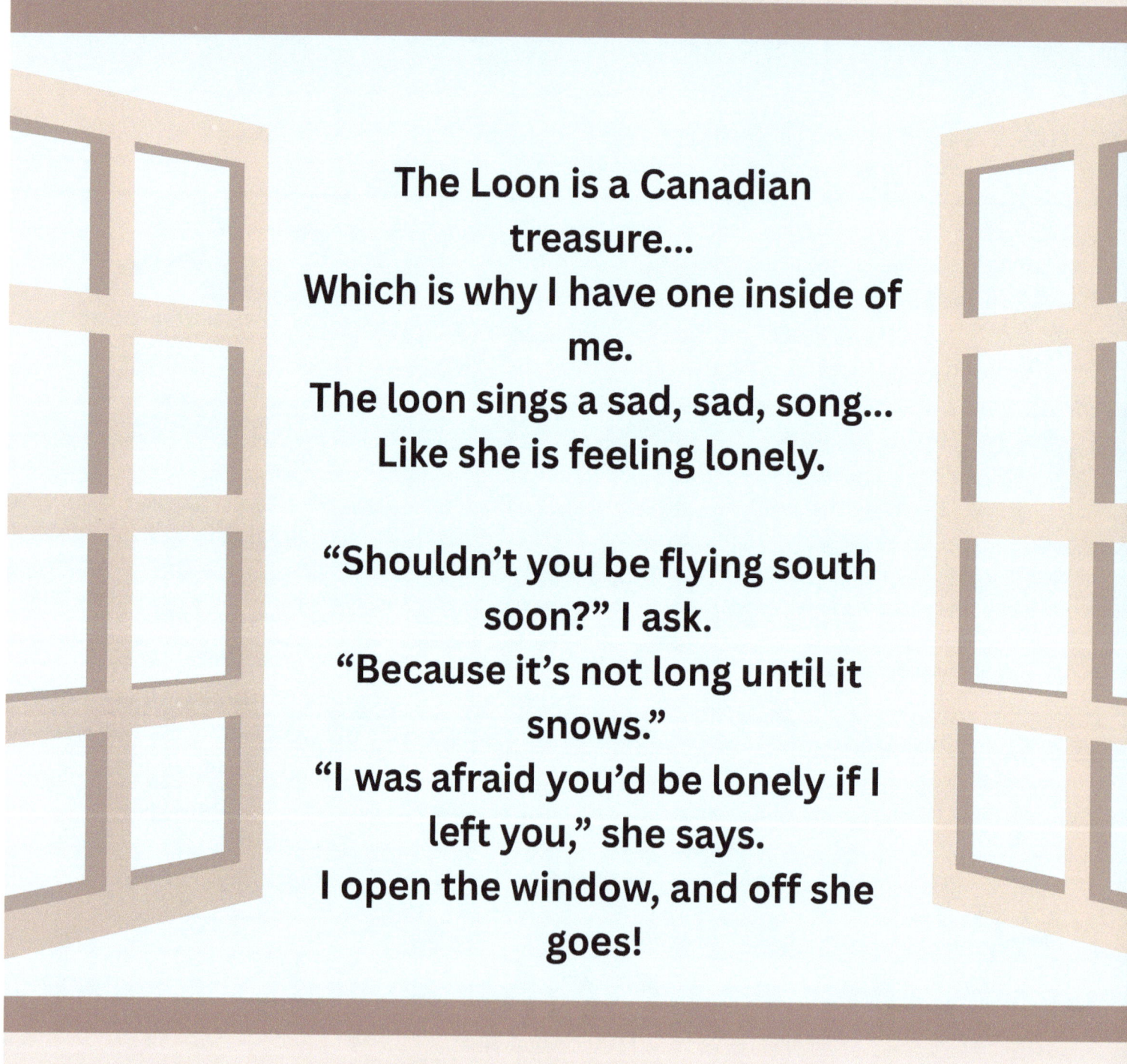

The Loon is a Canadian treasure...
Which is why I have one inside of me.
The loon sings a sad, sad, song...
Like she is feeling lonely.

"Shouldn't you be flying south soon?" I ask.
"Because it's not long until it snows."
"I was afraid you'd be lonely if I left you," she says.
I open the window, and off she goes!

CHRISTMAS BELLS

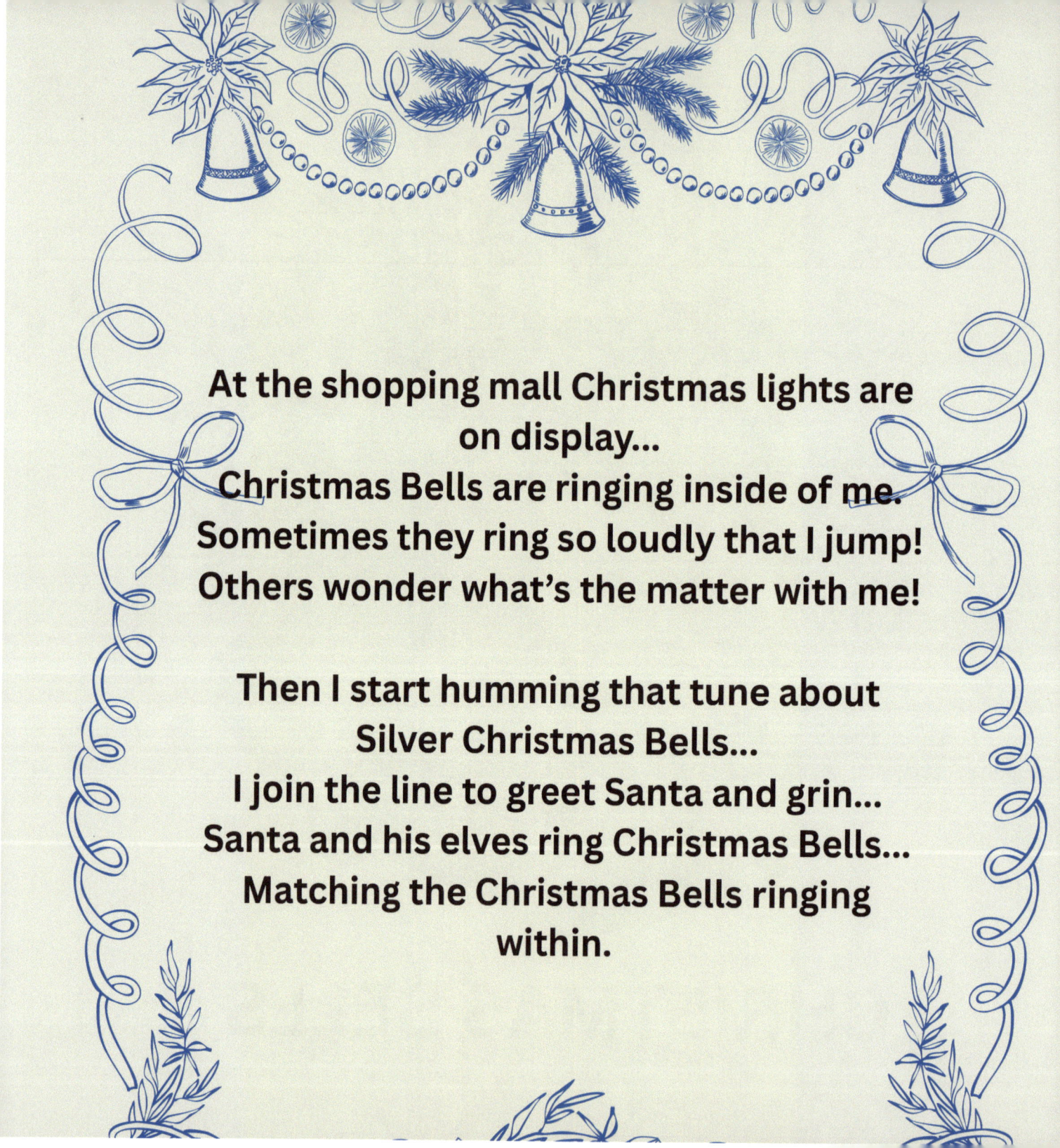

At the shopping mall Christmas lights are on display...
Christmas Bells are ringing inside of me.
Sometimes they ring so loudly that I jump!
Others wonder what's the matter with me!

Then I start humming that tune about Silver Christmas Bells...
I join the line to greet Santa and grin...
Santa and his elves ring Christmas Bells...
Matching the Christmas Bells ringing within.

Christmas spirit fills the world with harmony...
And with hope in our hearts for the future.
When the Christmas Bells ring inside of me...
I believe we'll find peace one day for sure!

peace on earth

SNOW GLOBE

I woke up with a trembling in my tummy!
There's a snow globe inside of me!
I don't even need to go outside!
Because snow is always falling inside me!

Then I have a strange urge to figure skate...
Even though I've never skated before - I'm able to...
I make sure I don't touch the snow globe walls...
They might smash or melt if I do!

I skate figure eights as the snow descends...
In this snow globe inside of me.
Soon the figure eights are covered in white...
I close my eyes in my bed and sleep soundly.

SNOW FLAKES

Snow flakes are fun to catch on my tongue!
Especially when there is all year snow inside of me!
"What are you doing?" my friend asks.
I say, "I'm catching snow flakes on my tongue! Watch me!"

"It's not right to tell lies," she replies.
It's not a lie - it's true but it's a truth I need to show.
I keep catching the snow flakes on my tongue.
And she begins catching them too just like so!

CHRISTMAS BLANKET

Once upon a time - Christmas was so much fun!
But now things are different for me...
Now all I want to do is cuddle up and hide...
In the blanket under the Christmas Tree.

It changed a few Christmas mornings ago...
When special occasions felt overwhelming to me.
So much attention, so many thank yous to say...
That's when I noticed the blanket hugging the tree.

The Christmas Tree itself was all lit up...
We'd decorated it magnificently!
And yet that blanket clung to it...
Holding it tightly, and unselfishly.

So, I imagined myself with that same blanket.
And now it lives inside of me.
Whenever I need a hug or a cuddle it knows...
And it throws its arms around me!

TOFU CHRISTMAS TURKEY

Christmas Day was once my favourite day!
I mean, of the entire year for me.
That was before Grandma went vegetarian...
And started serving Tofu Christmas Turkey!

Since then the Ghosts of Christmas past turkeys...
Have taken up inside of me.
They have given me a mission:
To destroy Grandma's Tofu Christmas Turkeys.

"I CAN'T!" I say to them.
"You WON'T!" they reply.
Then they beat their drumsticks high in the air!
Saying they won't stop until I comply!

To comply means to give in...
To their ghastly anti-tofu demands...
The Tofu Christmas Turkey wobbles like jelly...
We say "Yay Grandma!" and clap our hands!

Because The Chef - Grandma -
Is more loved than what I eat.
I sniff a little Tofu Christmas Turkey...
I'm not suprised it smells like feet!

The moral of my story is...
No matter what - we love our families.
One day we'll look back and laugh...
About Grandma's Tofu Christmas Turkey!

MY 🎁 POEM

MY POEM OR DRAWING

ALSO BY CATHY MCGOUGH

POETRY SERIES:

There's a Chimpanzee Inside of Me!
There's a Jumping Bean Inside of Me!

JUMP SERIES:

Jump Like a Caribou!
Jump Like a Kangaroo!
Jump at the Zoo!
Jump and Say P.U.!
Jump and Say Boo!
Jump and Say Valentine's Day Is
For Kids Too!
Jump and Look For a Clue!
Jump and Say Happy Birthday to You!
Jump For Everything Blue!
Jump, Hop and Say Happy Easter To You!
Jump and Say Cock-A-Doodle-Do!
Jump and Sing Da-Do-Do-Do!
Jump and Ask Who? Who?
Jump and Squawk Like a Cockatoo!
Jump and Ask Is It You or Ewe?
Jump and Say There's an Ewww in My Stew!
Jump and Say Merry Christmas To You!
Jump and Cheer Happy New Year!
Jump and Say There's a Moo-Moo in a Tutu!
Jump and Say There's a Hare in My Hair!
Jump and Say My Aunt Ate An Ant!
Jump and Say There's An Aardvark
In The Amusement Park!
Jump and Roar For The Dinosaurs!
Jump and Buzz Like A Bee!
Jump and Flutter Like A Butterfly!
Jump and Pop Like Popcorn!
Jump and Ribbit Like A Frog!
Jump and Snore Like A Koala!

Jump and Snuffle Like A Platypus!
Jump and Grunt Like A Groundhog!
Jump and Say Hello!
Jump and Say Friend!
Jump and Say Peace!
Jump and Say Sky!
Jump and Say Merry Christmas!
Jump and Say Happy New Year!
Jump and Say Fun!
Jump and Say Family!
Jump and Say Jump!

CLAP FOR SERIES:

Clap for 1!
Clap for 2!
Clap for 3!
Clap for 4!
Clap for 5!
Clap for 6!
Clap for 7!
Clap for 8!
Clap for 9!
Clap for 10!

The Cat Who Said Hello
The Three Boulders
Billy Shakespeare
Billie Shakespeare
Learn To Draw With Symmetry
ABC More Learn to Draw With Symmetry

Non-Fiction
103 Fundraising Ideas For Parent Volunteers With Schools and Teams

www.ingramcontent.com/pod-product-compliance
Lightning Source LLC
Chambersburg PA
CBHW041431120626
46547CB00002B/173